Oceans

By Christy Steele

STECK-VAUGHN
ELEMENTARY · SECONDARY · ADULT · LIBRARY

A Harcourt Company

www.steck-vaughn.com

ISBN 0-7398-4161-0

Library of Congress Cataloging-in-Publication Data is available upon request.

Printed and bound in the United States of America
10 9 8 7 6 5 4 3 2 1 W 04 03 02 01

Photo Acknowledgments
Photo credits:
Corbis/Stephen Frink, 8; Bill Ross, 10; Lester V. Bergman, 15; Jeffrey L. Rotman, 16, 18; Douglas P. Wilson/Frank Land Picture Agency, 20; Brandon D. Cole, 25; AFP, 28; Digital Stock Photos, title page, 5, 12, 22, 26 Photo Network/Scott Winer, cover

Contents

The killer whale has adapted so it can live in cold ocean water.

THE OCEANS BIOME

Some scientists study parts of Earth called biomes. Biomes are large regions, or areas, that have communities of plants and animals. A community is a group of plants and animals that live in the same place. Oceans are a biome.

Each biome has a different climate. Climate is the usual weather in a place. Climate includes wind speeds, amount of rainfall, and temperature. Temperature measures how hot or cold a place is.

Different biomes have different kinds of soils. Many kinds of plants grow in biomes with rich soil. Fewer plants grow in biomes with dry, poor, or wind-blown soil.

Plants and animals are **adapted** to their biomes. To be adapted means that a living thing has features that help it fit where it lives.

Continents
Oceans

The Ocean

The ocean biome is the largest biome in the world. Oceans, or huge bodies of water, cover 71% of Earth. There are three main oceans and one smaller ocean. The four oceans are the Pacific, Atlantic, Indian, and Arctic. All the oceans join to make one large ocean.

The Pacific Ocean is the largest ocean. On its western side are Asia and Australia. On its eastern side are North and South America. The Pacific Ocean covers about 70 million square miles (181 million sq. km). The Pacific is the deepest ocean. It is an average of about 14,000 feet (4,267 m) deep.

The Atlantic Ocean lies between North and South America and Europe and Africa. It covers about 41 million square miles (106 million sq. km). The Atlantic is an average of about 12,257 feet (3,736 m) deep.

The Indian Ocean lies between Africa and Australia. It covers about 28 million square miles (73.5 million sq. km). Its average is about 13,000 feet (3,962 m) deep.

The Arctic is the smallest and shallowest ocean. It covers about 5.4 million square miles (14 million sq. km). It is an average of about 4,300 feet (1,311 m) deep. The Arctic Ocean lies in the north polar areas. It is the coldest ocean.

 This fish and colorful coral live in the sunlit zone.

Ocean Zones

Scientists divide the ocean into regions. Regions are then divided into parts called zones. Zones can be divided by depth, or how deep they are. They can also be divided by how far they are from land or how much sunlight they receive. Different plants and animals have adapted to live in each ocean zone.

Different zones receive different amounts of sunlight. The water gets darker and colder as it gets deeper.

The sunlit zone is the upper zone. It begins at the ocean's surface and goes down 490 feet (150 m). Sunlight brightens and heats water most in this zone. About 90% of ocean plants and animals live in the sunlit zone.

The twilight zone stretches from 490 feet (150 m) to 3,280 feet (1,000 m) deep. Not much sunlight reaches the twilight zone. The water is colder and darker. Fish live in the twilight zone, but not many plants can live there.

The midnight zone is the deepest zone. It stretches from below 3,280 feet (1,000 m) to the ocean floor. No light reaches the midnight zone. It is completely dark and very cold. Very few animals and plants live there.

Ocean coasts are places where a continental plate and an oceanic plate meet.

About Oceans

Earth is made up of three parts. The center of the planet is a metal and rock core. A layer of heavy rocks called the mantle surrounds the core. Parts of the mantle are molten, or melted, rock. The crust is the thin, rocky outer layer of the planet.

Earth's crust is divided into giant pieces called plates. Some plates carry thick continental crust. Other plates carry thinner oceanic crust. The thinner ocean crust sits lower on the plates than continental crust. Water covers the lower areas.

Plates move. They slide over molten rock in the mantle. New ocean crust is formed when some plates move apart. Ocean crust is destroyed when some plates crash together.

The Hawaiian Islands are volcano tops. Hot steam is blowing out of this volcano in Hawaii.

The Ocean Floor

Dry land has many different features. For example, there are mountains, valleys, and plains. The ocean floor also has as many different features as dry land. There are mountains. Some are so tall, they rise above the surface of the ocean. There are long, narrow valleys with steep walls. These deep valleys are called **trenches**. The deepest trench is the Mariana Trench in the Pacific Ocean. It is 36,198 feet (11,033 m) deep. If Mount Everest was in the Mariana Trench, it would still have water covering its top. There are also huge, flat areas on the ocean floor called **abyssal plains**. Many mountains and hills rise from the ocean floor. Mountains form when melted rock pushes its way through the ocean floor and piles up. Many mountains found in the ocean are taller than mountains on land.

Some ocean mountains are volcanoes. Volcanoes are vents in the Earth's surface. Sometimes volcanoes become so tall that they rise above the water. The tops of these volcanoes become islands. The Hawaiian Islands are the tops of volcanoes.

Some volcanoes below the surface of the water were once above it. Wind and rain wore them down. Water levels rose and covered the volcanoes. These volcanoes are called **seamounts**. Waves wear down some seamounts even more until they have flat tops. A flat-topped seamount is called a guyot.

Water and Sediments

Ocean water is saltwater. About 3.5% of ocean water is made up of salt.

Sediments cover the ocean floor. Sediments are tiny pieces of soil, sand, and dead plant and animal material. Water washes some of these things from land into the ocean. Other things are already in the ocean. The materials that form sediment settle on the ocean floor.

There are many tiny organisms, or living things, in the oceans. Some of these organisms make shells. When the organisms die, their shells fall to the ocean floor. They become part of the sediment. When sediment has lots of shells in it, it is called **ooze**.

Currents

Currents are streams of moving water. In the ocean, currents form when wind blows over the surface. The wind pushes and pulls on the water. Other currents move up and down in the ocean.

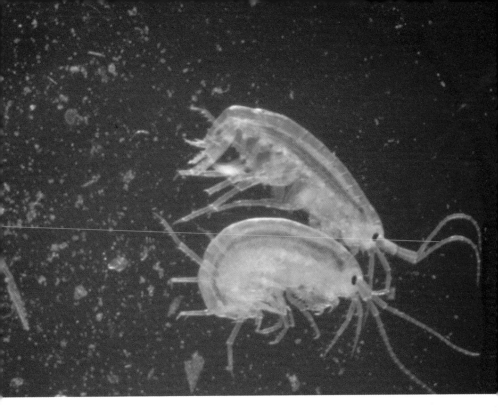

These tiny ocean animals have shells. Their shells will become part of ooze after they die.

Some currents are warm, and some are cold. Some currents flow deep in the ocean, and some flow near the surface. Currents carry warm and cool water around the world.

This is a close-up view of soft coral feeding on plankton.

Ocean Plants

P lants need sunlight and nutrients to live. A nutrient is something that helps living things grow. Ocean plants need nutrients from ocean water to grow. Plants use sunlight to make food in a process called photosynthesis. That is why most ocean plants live close to the surface. Many plants live in shallow water near coasts.

Plankton are organisms that float or drift in water. **Phytoplankton** are one-celled floating or drifting plants. They are too tiny for people to see. They do not have any roots. They float close to the surface. Ocean currents carry phytoplankton around certain parts of the ocean. Many fish eat phytoplankton as food.

Since sunlight shines through water, kelp plants can perform photosynthesis to grow.

How Ocean Plants Survive

Ocean plants have adapted to living in water. Some ocean plants have roots or other ways to keep them from floating away. Some plants have flowers like plants on land. The flowers make pollen. Pollen are cells that plants need to make new plants. On land, insects and wind carry pollen from one plant to another. In the ocean, water carries pollen to other plants.

There are more than 50 kinds of seagrass. Seagrass grows near coasts. Roots hold seagrass to rocks or sediment. Seagrass often grows in huge fields. Many animals live in seagrass fields.

Algae grow in oceans. Algae are small plants without roots or stems that grow in wet places. Algae can grab rocks or the ocean floor to stay in place. Algae need sunlight for photosynthesis. They have small air-filled sacs that help them float near the surface.

Kelp is a common kind of ocean algae. There are many different kinds of kelp. Some kinds can grow more than 100 feet (30.5 m) long. Many kelp grow together near coasts. They form huge kelp forests.

FUN FACT

Mangroves are trees that grow in saltwater. Mangroves have huge webs of roots that stretch above ground and below ground. The roots hold the trees in place.

This is an adult jellyfish. Newly hatched jellyfish are part of zooplankton.

Ocean Animals

Many different kinds of animals live in oceans. Scientists think there are ocean animals they have not found yet. They think many of these animals might live deep in the ocean.

The tiniest ocean animals are **zooplankton**. Zooplankton are a mix of many different kinds of floating animals. The mix includes newly hatched fish, jellyfish, and crustaceans. Crustaceans are animals with outer shells. Crabs and shrimp are examples of crustaceans. Zooplankton float close to the surface and eat phytoplankton. Zooplankton are food for thousands of kinds of small fish.

Dolphins are mammals that have adapted to live in the ocean.

Fish and Mammals

About 20,000 different kinds of fish live in the ocean. Scientists separate fish into two groups. The larger group includes fish with jaws. Fish in the other group do not have jaws. Some fish spend their lives at one depth. Other fish swim from depth to depth to find food.

A **mammal** is a warm-blooded animal with a backbone. Mammals make milk to feed their young. Mammals have lungs and need to breathe air. Most mammals live on land. Whales and dolphins are mammals that live in oceans.

How Ocean Animals Live

Most living things need oxygen to live. Dissolved oxygen gas is in water. To dissolve is to seem to disappear when mixed with liquid. Fish have special body parts called gills. Gills take out the dissolved oxygen from water so fish can breathe it.

Mammals that live in oceans have no gills. They have blowholes on the tops of their bodies. They swim to the surface and breathe through their blowholes. Their blowholes are closed underwater.

The bodies of many ocean animals help them move through water. Most have pointed heads that help them cut through water. They have fins to help them change direction. They have tails that move back and forth to help push them through water.

How Ocean Animals Have Adapted

Ocean animals have ways to keep safe. Some fish are dark on top and light on bottom. The different colors make it harder for predators, or animals that eat other animals, to see them in the water. Flying fish have two large side fins. When they are chased by a predator, they jump out of the water and glide through air. A pufferfish blows up its body to look larger to frighten away a predator.

Fish that live deep in the ocean must find food without light. It can be hard to find food in the dark. Most fish deep in the ocean are less than 12 inches (30 cm) long. Larger fish would need more food to live.

Some fish have special ways of finding food. The angler fish has a stringlike rod at the top of its head. The end of the string glows. The angler eats fish that swim toward the glow.

FUN FACT Many kinds of plants and animals live in special places called coral reefs. A reef is made of small skeletons of animals called corals.

The flying fish uses its winglike fins to glide through the air after it jumps out of water.

Some animals live on the ocean floor. The tripod fish has fins that stop it from sinking into the sediment. Giant worms live under the sediment. They swallow it. Their bodies use bits of food in the sediment.

Hurricanes are huge storms that form over oceans. Hurricanes have swirling winds and cause heavy rain. They can cause floods and blow down houses if they strike land.

Oceans and People

The ocean can be dangerous for people. Strong storms and huge waves sink boats. Storms that begin over oceans can flood land.

Long ago, people thought the world was flat. They thought that people could sail off the edge of the ocean. They also thought huge sea monsters lived in oceans.

Today, people know more about oceans. Ships called submarines travel underwater. People who dive use special equipment to breathe underwater. Some scientists use computers and other tools to study plants and animals in the ocean. Others study the mountains, valleys, water, and sediments.

 This bird was coated with oil after a boat leaked oil into the ocean.

Overfishing

People catch ocean fish for food. Scientists worry that people are overfishing. Overfishing happens when people catch too many of one kind of fish. Then, new fish cannot have enough young to replace the fish that have been caught.

Overfishing can endanger some sea animals. Endanger means in danger of dying out. Since 1950, the number of fish caught each year has grown so much that some kinds of fish and whales are endangered.

Pollution

Pollution also hurts the ocean. Pollution is harmful material that is added to air, water, or soil. It can kill ocean plants and animals.

Oil spills are one kind of ocean pollution. Boats carrying oil sometimes leak or sink. Spilled oil floats to the surface. The oil coats seabirds, making it difficult for them to move. It coats the fur of animals like otters. This makes it hard for the animals to stay warm. Oil spills hurt fish and other animals, too. Most of these animals die.

Future of Oceans

Some people are working to study and save oceans. Some are trying to make laws to protect oceans and the plants and animals that live in them. These people are working to keep oceans safe for the future.

Glossary

abyssal plain (uh-BISS-uhl PLANE)—the flat part of the ocean floor

adapt (uh-DAPT)—to change over time to fit in a special environment

algae (AL-jee)—plantlike life without roots, stems, or leaves; algae live in or under water.

mammal (MAM-uhl)—a warm-blooded animal with a backbone; mammals breathe air.

ooze (OOZ)—soft mud on the ocean floor that contains a great deal of shells

phytoplankton (phye-toh-PLANGK-ton)—very tiny, one-celled plants that float in water

pollute (puh-LOOT)—to make dirty or unfit with waste

seamount (SEE-mount)—an underwater volcano

trench (TRENCH)—a deep crack in the ocean floor

zooplankton (zoo-PLANGK-ton)—a mix of many different kinds of floating animals

Internet Sites

Oceans Alive
http://www.abc.net.au/oceans/alive.htm

Secrets@Sea
http://www.secretsatsea.org

Useful Addresses

Office of Oceanic and Atmospheric Research
Silver Spring Metro Center
Building 3, Room 11627
1315 East-West Highway
Silver Spring, MD 20910

U.S. Environmental Protection Agency
Office of Water
Ariel Rios Building
1200 Pennsylvania Avenue, NW
Washington, DC 20460

INDEX